A **Pr⬧fit**
to Her Husband

Prophet

Dr. Melinda Harper

Dr. Melinda Harper

Published by
Bravin Publishing, LLC
PO Box 340317
Jamaica, New York
www.bravinpublishing.com

ISBN-13 978-0-9905377-1-7
Library of Congress Control Number 2015934211

Cover Design by Marisa Britton

Printed in the United States of America

Acknowledgments

With special thanks:

To the Lord, for trusting me with this book and giving me loving and gentle reminders that the words written in these pages are not mine, but Yours. Thank You for nudging me, as only You know how, and sending people, sometimes total strangers, who would also speak life into this book.

To my family, who is a constant encouraging team. You all, Broderick, Kennedy, and Broderick II, are always there cheering me on in everything I do. If it weren't for your love, patience and encouragement, I would not have been able to do this project with confidence.

To my Apostle Ricky D. Floyd and his wife, Pastor Sheila Floyd, thank you for being transparent in your marriage so that we could see what real Christian love looks like. Your unwavering love and dedication to holy, happy, healthy marriages is a great example for many. Thank you for giving birth to The School of Marriage Enhancement, which taught me how to be a wife.

A very special thanks to my husband, Broderick Harper! I love you. After all we have said and done, and all we are going to say and do, I want to say that I am not just happy to be married to you. I am honored to be your wife. I will strive daily to be your "Good Thing" and be a profit and prophet to you!

Contents

Foreword

A Profit/Prophet to Her Husband is going to bless many women of many backgrounds, especially those who truly desire to be that blessing, and that helpmate to their husbands. Times have changed, cultures have evolved, and a woman's mantle, I should say, has been varied in so many ways. Being a *profit* to our husbands means we aren't willing to walk the line of an uncertain society, but follow the guidance that was inbred in us before we were ever born. We have all the equipment necessary to make the title of this book real in our own lives...sadly, for many women, this realization has been hindered by tragedy.

The words in this book will allow us all to remember that no matter how inept we feel, no matter how we were raised, no matter how physically or emotionally battered down we've become, we have the power to rise from the debris of the past, and be a *prophetic* word—an encouraging and uplifting word—to a man who sees, endures, and carries so much. There are so many distractions in the world that depicts how a woman should be, what we should desire when our world seems displeasing to us, but when you have a woman of wisdom, such as this author, on your side helping you to be fierce and content with who you are, a displeasing life can become a satisfying life. We have the power to change it. Many of us don't believe we do, but the abilities are all there.

Dr. Melinda Harper

When I think about it, a book like this is not simply a book, but a tool of discovery like the archaeologists used to find hidden treasures that were already in the earth. The treasures your husband seeks are within you, waiting to be discovered by you first, and enjoyed by him, until death do you part. Understanding who you are, and the powers you truly possess will no doubt change the way you see every-thing … and when your perspective changes, everything around you does, too. So, take hold of this amazing piece of knowledge in your hands and be reminded of the fact that you can be a tremendous help to your husband despite what you've endured and suffered because the Lord can heal you and *still* make you a Profit/Prophet to *Your* Husband.

-S. M. Phelon

Author of *"The reNEWed Girl"*

Introduction

Are You Ready To Be a Wife?

he purpose of this book is to help wives understand who they are and who they were designed to be. Not every woman will become a wife. So this book is not for every woman. This book is for wives only. If you are not a wife yet, but desire to be, there is another book I have written that is just for you. It is especially for those women who want to be married and desire to have a husband. It will ultimately help you decide if you desire to be a wife (or not).

If you are single, having never been married, I caution you about reading this. There are things in this book that could scare you about becoming a wife, only because you may not fully understand its reference points. The best way to describe it is this. If you were to discuss with a woman who did not have children, all the *joys* of being a mom, including wiping snot with your own shirt, staying up late at night with a sick child, and all those other motherly pleasures, there are some things, she just would not understand or even find joyful at all. Understandingly, until you are fully immersed in parenting, there is just no way to fully comprehend it.

The same goes for marriage and being a wife. Until you are married, or were once married, there are some things you just will not understand. If my warning has not been enough, then keep reading, but don't say I didn't warn you. Either way, I know you will get some valuable information that you can use and refer back to later.

Until you are married and fully immersed in being a wife, there is no real way to comprehend what it is, even by reading it. You just have to trust me on this. The only reason wives will understand this is because they live it daily and they have either lived some of what I will discuss, or they are currently living it.

I have had single friends with whom I have been very open with about being a wife. Each one at different points would shake her head at some of the things I'd share and directly say, "No, that

won't be me." A few of those same friends, after being married for as short as one month, called, crying and saying, "Why didn't you tell me…" and I replied, "I did! Remember, you said it wouldn't be you."

I am, in no way, gloating that what I told them would happen, happened. I am merely making the point that they were not able to see what I really meant until they were wives themselves. One statement I distinctly remember one friend saying to me after I told her that marriage was work:

"Marriage is only work for the ones who are failing at it."

I will leave her name unmentioned. However, I laughed so hard I was in tears. I know at the time she probably thought I was delusional, because she looked at me with a puzzled look on her face and kept talking, and I kept laughing. I could only dream that were a true statement. That was the best laugh of the night. Now that she is married, she sees the hard truth. She sees the work that has to be done, and it has nothing to do with a failing marriage. We both laugh at that statement now. It has become our inside joke. Now when we speak and I ask, "How are things going?" her reply is, "We're working on it."

Like a garden, marriage has to be cultivated, cared for, watered, fertilized, weeded, and pruned. It is work if you want a healthy, beautiful garden and no less hard work if you desire a healthy, beautiful, productive, fruitful marriage.

Another misconception single women have is about their willingness to have sex once they were married. One single woman swore that she would never get tired of it. If you have single friends, just humor yourself and ask them what they think their sex life will be once they are married. They can't imagine not wanting to have sex, or not being in the mood to please their fleshly desires with the man of their dreams. I would venture to say that's because right now, they are not obligated to. One dear friend said that she would be ready for him whenever, however, and wherever. I strongly encouraged that, and was happy to hear she had that aspiration. I prayed it would remain with her well after the first couple months of getting married. Needless to say, the feeling of wanting to have sex all the time was short lived. It dissipated after the first few disagreements over whose job it was to cook, do laundry, and take the cat to the vet. Feeling appreciated increases the sex drive, but I'll discuss this later.

If you are single, and shaking your head, and thinking you will *not* be like my friend, sex will not become scarce just because you had an argument, then maybe you *should* read this book. Maybe you will be able to head off some of the pitfalls we married women have made and fallen into. Once you are married, it is an entirely different ball game; sex is not only for pleasure, but for keeping the oneness on track. Sex is much more, and it should be pleasurable. I am getting ahead of myself; so let me get back to the purpose of the book.

For women who are currently wives, it cannot be stressed, enough.

This book is for YOU!

Just for clarification, a live-in girlfriend is not a wife. A longtime mistress is not a wife. A fiancée is not a wife. A wife is commonly defined as a female partner in a continuing *marital* relationship. This is meaningful when looking at the Bible's definition of a wife.

The first Biblical reference to a wife is found in Genesis 2:21-25. When God made a woman from Adam's rib and presented her to Adam, the first marriage was established.

²¹ And the LORD God caused a deep sleep to fall upon Adam, and he slept: and he took one of his ribs, and closed up the flesh instead thereof;

²² And the rib, which the LORD God had taken from man, made he a woman, and brought her unto the man.

²³ And Adam said, This is now bone of my bones, and flesh of my flesh: she shall be called Woman, because she was taken out of Man.

²⁴ Therefore shall a man leave his father and his mother, and shall cleave unto his wife: and they shall be one flesh.

²⁵ And they were both naked, the man and his wife, and were not ashamed.

Single women often approach me with their desires to "be married." When a single woman says, "I want to be married" or "I want a husband," my immediate response is:

"Are you ready to be a wife?"

I have gotten some strange looks for saying this. However, as a wife, you already know what I mean. Being a wife is not for the faint of heart. As I said before, it is work. Just so that we are clear on my stance, being married and being a wife are not one and the same. I guess you picked up on that.

When a woman says she wants to be "married," she is thinking about how marriage will benefit her. Let's be honest. We didn't desire marriage thinking of all the ways we would be a benefit to our husbands. When we declared we wanted a husband, it was for the purposes of him helping us. There was something about having a husband that sounded appealing. I have heard lots of reasons women say they want to be married, or they want a husband. I heard one woman say that having a husband meant she would have someone to keep her gas tank filled, and she would not have to pump her own gas anymore. Well, where did she ever get that idea? Maybe her father kept her mom's gas tank filled. Wherever she got it from, her husband was not part of that, and as a result, the first time she didn't have her tank filled, she was disappointed. I heard another woman in exasperation say that she had gotten married because she wanted to have someone always home with her. Someone she could share things with and laugh with. For her, having a husband was more of wanting a live-in best friend and companion. Someone there so she would not have to be alone. When her husband had to work late, or he chose to go out with the guys instead of staying home with her and watching television and laughing at reruns, she suddenly felt unloved. This was not what she thought having a husband would be like. Her dream of having a husband was shattered.

Having a husband for some may have meant help with the bills, for others it may have meant help the kids, the car, or to relieve some sexual urges. I have heard many reasons why women want to be married. For whatever reasons we really wanted to be married and wanted a husband, for most of us, it was not what it turned out to be. In many cases, it was far more than what we bargained for. I believe so many marriages are ending up in divorce because of what we perceive marriage should be and a husband should act like. We jumped into it without any real knowledge of what to expect or the expectations we had were unrealistic. Frankly, some of us were not concerned about the job description. We were more concerned with the title and status of being married and being called someone's wife. Now we realize the title is not worth it. It is a difficult and challenging assignment that we were not fully prepared or equipped for. After all, I wanted a husband; I didn't consider that he wanted a wife and what that included. Looking back, I am undeniably certain I didn't even know what that meant.

We find ourselves asking why. Why did I get married? Why me, God? Being married isn't what I thought it would be. Soon after "I do," many of us realized that we signed up for a role we had not been properly prepared for. We were now wives with no official training. Having a husband looked so good from the single side of life. Remember how you would look at a couple and dream about the day you too would have a husband? Did you ever look at a couple and dream about the day you were going to be *your* husband's helper? Did you visualize balancing the books, the babies and the bedroom? If you are like me, you did not. I did not have a clue what it meant to be a wife. I only wanted to be married and have a husband! That all looked good enough for me to jump right on in.

Being a wife is not a part-time job. It's not just for the good times, as a girlfriend can rightfully choose. It's not the hopes and dreams the fiancée may have of living their lives happily ever after. Being a wife is full-time, every day, through every instance, and with all your heart in it kind of job. You don't get to go home when he starts to get on your nerves. (This is one of the things I told my single friend, and she insisted she would never want to leave him). I most

13

cases, you don't get to take a few days alone to catch a breather when he begins to demand too much. You are not afforded the opportunity to take a relationship break for a while because things are getting too complicated or too serious.

Being a wife is being able to see the worst in the person you love the most, and still being able to love and respect him.

This is only one characteristic of a wife. Being a wife also means being able to heal those broken places in your husband that you didn't even know were broken, while praying in the midst that your broken places be healed. Being an intercessor for him even though you have needs of your own. That is what a wife is.

Marriage is more than a partnership or contractual agreement. In a contractual agreement, there is "consideration given for consideration received." In other words, I do because you do. I agree to_____ because you agree to _____. We agree, and that is the premise of the partnership and/or contract. On the other hand, if either party breaks the agreement, we know that we can call it off.

Well, marriage is NOT that! Marriage is a covenant. The Bible says, "So they are no longer two but one flesh. What therefore God has joined together, let no one separate" (Matthew 19:6). Marriage is giving of one's self—regardless of the return value. Both parties do not always maintain their promises. Either spouse may have fallen short of meeting his or her full obligations, but do you get to call it quits? Throw the baby out with the bathwater? No. You still do your part as a wife. You maintain your integrity, and God will honor your sacrifices. When you fall short, repent and get back up, and do better. Your role as a wife has a bigger purpose.

First, my being a wife is for the purpose of my husband. It's that plain and simple. Your being a wife is for the purpose of your husband. Every wife is specifically designed for the husband she agreed to marry. She is uniquely created as an individual, and as a wife. You were chosen first by God, then by your husband. You are not a wife by accident or by luck. The Lord chose you because He could trust you with a husband. He trusts you to help him when he needs help. He trusts you to protect his heart. He trusts you to stay when times get hard. He trusts you with your husband's dreams, his future and his very life! You are a wife because you could be trusted with the husband He chose for you. If you knew all this prior to marriage, would you still say, "I want a husband?" I know I would have thought a bit harder and longer about if I wanted to be wife or not. Having a husband is a lot of work and responsibility. Now that I am married and I have learned what my role is as a wife, I have accepted that I am a wife for a reason.

YOU ARE A WIFE FOR A REASON!

In the past, when I questioned myself about why I got married, I was left with no answer. Now, that I have knowledge about what it means to be married, I only have to remind myself that I have an ordained assignment and purpose as a wife that is blessed by the hand of God.

God created marriage, so when I feel overwhelmed with being a wife, I can go to Him for guidance, comfort and answers. Remember, you have everything in you to be a wife. There were qualities about you, prior to marriage that made you a wife, and your husband recognized it, and you were found. You are a wife, and a good thing, not just a married woman.

Here is a prayer you can pray when you need to be reassured about your assignment.

Write in your husband's name if you want.

I am _____ 's wife for a
                    Husband's Name
reason.

I am uniquely created to help meet his needs like no other woman can. I was created for a purpose. I was made with
_____ in mind.
       Husband's Name
I am exactly what he needs. I was created according to those needs, and I am a profit, as well as a prophet, to my husband. God has entrusted me to be the chosen helper for His son.
In me, _____ has found a good
          Husband's Name
thing, and favor in God. We are one, and no one can separate us.

AMEN.

Now that we have affirmed who we are, and that we were created with purpose and a plan, hopefully we can begin the journey of uncovering how we are to be a profit and a prophet to our husbands. Enjoy this book, and refer back to it as often as you need or desire. I pray blessings over every person who reads this book. I pray that your relationships are prosperous, and bear much fruit for endless seasons to come.

So it shall be!

Dr. Melinda Harper

CHAPTER ONE

Mirror, Mirror

*Look in the mirror,
What do you see?
A stranger standing there...
Looking at me!*

W hy should you recognize the woman in the mirror if you haven't engaged yourself with this woman intimately? The woman in the poem ends by saying there is a stranger looking back at her. The crazy thing is...she just might be right! *"Who is that woman?"*

She is soignee, the manifested talent of a universal creator. She is elegantly and magnificently made. However, if you have but lost the connection with her, just know that this woman, in her purest form, wants to reconnect with you. She is the inner you.

Yes, I am speaking in metaphors here, but even the Bible talks about the importance of being of one mind. Yet when we are torn, and we harden our hearts to the Holy Spirit's promptings, we cause a spiritual division within ourselves called instability. We become unstable in our ways, and in our thinking (James 1:8).

Some women don't want to face the mirror because living in ignorance means, "I don't have to face the discomfort of change." Ignorance can be blissful at times! However, this woman, your soul, your authentic

19

self, yearns for you to know her. She wants to be one with you. She also yearns to walk with you, to express the love of God with you. Your soul no more likes to be left alone in the forgotten shadows than you do. But here, your soul is at your mercy, letting you have the wheel.

The Holy Spirit should be our guide if we desire to stay on the right road, at the right pace, in the right lane. Sure, we've been in a few "car accidents" ourselves, but our car is not totaled. We can drive it again, and so can you. What I am saying is this: yes, you've been abused, molested, or abandoned. You've been taken advantage of, looked over, or treated unfairly. You've been lied on or lied to, cheated on, and sometimes forced into situations that were uncomfortable. You have been bruised, but not broken. Broken, but not shattered. You have not been destroyed. No weapon formed against you shall ever be able to prosper (Isaiah 54:17).

Any car that has not been totaled (terminated indefinitely) is taken to an auto body shop for repairs and then put back on the road. God will not put on us more than we can bear (1 Corinthians 10:13), so we need not worry about being destroyed. We need to start rejoicing in being repaired. The Lord brings restoration through His love. He also shows us how to perform self-care upon ourselves through accepting ourselves, thinking godly, speaking positive, and renewing our minds. His Word says "And be not conformed to this world: but be ye transformed by the renewing of your mind, that ye may prove what [is] that good, and acceptable, and perfect, will of God" (Romans 12:2). He does this so we can get back on the road to becoming healthy and whole to serve His purpose. We are not here for ourselves; we have a much greater purpose that we are called and commanded to do.

Not all women have an unhealthy or distorted view of who they truly are, and they are determined, motivated, and compassionate women. While this book will discuss the struggles some women have with accepting themselves, there are some women who are overly indulgent in self. This book can serve as a tool for women to (1) encourage those who regularly deal with low self-esteem or un-acceptance and (2) shine some light on the destructive path that self-obsession can bring.

Satan has been woman's adversary since tricking Eve in the garden. Therefore, from the beginning of your birth, he has been devising ways to destroy you by distorting your view of who you really are. Picture a woman straining to look out of a closed window to see an image on the road. She lifts the window, and from out of nowhere, a bird swoops down in her line of sight, making it difficult for her to see. Next, a gust of wind brings all manner of floating debris into her eyes. Once she wipes it away, flying paper whips around her face, continuously whipping one right after another. She returns the window to its closed position and sits in her chair. She gives up trying to see what the image was on the road. After a while, she doesn't even wonder.

Since the enemy cannot destroy us outright, he sends distractions in the form of people and situations to blind or distort our view. The enemy's plan is that you would be immobilized by rape and abuse, that you would be severely hindered by a cheating or lying spouse. But the devil is a liar! The Father knows how powerful love and forgiveness is. He understands the abuses we've suffered because He has suffered...*and far worse than any of us can imagine.* He said *(and I am paraphrasing)* if I can endure such a suffering, and still grant [them] permission to nail me to a cross with the expectation to forgive each and every one of them, then surely (for Me) you can find it in yourself to forgive and let not My suffering be in vain.

The Father is not heartless, He gives us a season to grieve and a season to be sad, but there is an expectation to move on in confidence with His promises of healing. Here are a few scriptures to start the healing process.

Psalm 147:3

He heals the brokenhearted, and binds up their wounds.

Jeremiah 30:17

For I will restore health unto you, and I will heal you of your wounds, saith the Lord.

Proverbs 3:7-8

Do not be wise in your own eyes; fear the Lord and depart from evil. It will be health to your flesh, and strength to your bones.

LOVE THYSELF

I've mentioned some of the deeper issues women face when it comes to their self-esteem. Such things as molestation, rape, physical abuse ...but on a different note, we can agree that we've heard our share of stories about women disliking their physical appearance...present company included. This just might be the most common struggle women of all ages, races, and creed have dealt with since the beginning of time. It's obvious to me that Eve thought there was something about herself that was not quite good enough...that something was missing...that if she had a little more of this or a little more of that, she would be better off. That's part of the problem, ladies. We don't see ourselves the way Christ sees us; therefore, our Christ-esteem is not fully developed.

{

Quick Thought
A genuine love for yourself will transition
into a genuine love for others.

}

Psalm 30:2

Oh Lord my God, I cried unto thee and thou hast healed me.

23

Christ-esteem is seeing ourselves the way God sees us. We are made in His image and likeness (Genesis 1:27). So, we should remind ourselves daily that God made us exactly the way He wants us to be. In comparing ourselves to others, we develop a warped sense of *self*-esteem. How do you compare two perfect creatures? God uniquely designed each of us, so there is no comparison. A genuine love for self will transition into a genuine love for others.

The phrase says to *love thyself*: mind, body and spirit. This is important to do because each of these areas is an entity that must be nurtured. While they may be an entity unto themselves, they are connected in very profound ways. They are connected spiritually. They each affect one another in very real ways. One way to bring harmony to the mind, body and spirit is love. In order to be a prophet and a profit to your husband, you must first *love thyself*. You are your first ministry. Yes, a woman can serve others in a broken and injured state, but what would that benefit a marriage covenant if the two cannot become one?

An unacceptable, unwholesome past life can cause women to feel unlovable toward themselves. The heart becomes an incubator for bitterness, resentment, and unforgiveness. This (stained) heart follows her throughout her life and taints everything she touches. Healing and restoration must take place in order for you to be able to operate in your giftedness of being a wife. No matter what your husband does or says, you will only filter it thorough a hurt, broken lens. The image will be distorted. Your Christ-esteem has to be rebuilt in order for you to see yourself the way Christ sees you, and ultimately for you to see your husband the way Christ sees him.

Ask Yourself

1. How has my past contributed to my present self-image?

   _____

   _____

   _____

   _____

2. What lies from the enemy have kept me from loving myself and seeing my self as made in God's image?

   _____

   _____

   _____

   _____

3. What am I willing to do to build up my Christ-esteem?

   _____

   _____

   _____

   _____

Lord,

Show me how to love and take care of myself. Where the enemy has come in and fed me lies, replace those lies with Your truth about who I am. I am fearfully and wonderfully made. Help me to come into agreement with Your Word. Give me wisdom about what I should wear, how I should adorn myself, and how I should treat my body. I am Your perfect creation, created in Your image. I am beautiful, I am the right shape, I am the right size, I have the right complexion, I am beautiful in every way, and may others see the beauty of You reflected in me.

Mirror, Mirror

ADDITIONAL NOTES:

_____

_____

_____

_____

_____

_____

_____

_____

_____

CHAPTER TWO

The Quarrelsome Wife

nhealthy words can be just as potent as a deadly poison or a toxic acid. They enter the heart and break down our structure until all the life is extracted. Unwholesome words can only come from a heart that is already toxic. If our words are full of contempt, bitterness, and un-forgiveness, the only outcome will be someone getting hurt, or someone's spirit being murdered. I know this sounds gruesome, and drastic; however, it is the truth. Speaking this way not only hurts the relationship, but it also hurts you emotionally and physically.

Dwelling with a quarrelsome wife is such a depressing place to be that a man would rather take his chances "living on a rooftop" or with another woman. The dictionary says that a quarrelsome woman (person) is a controversial person, someone who simply likes to arouse controversy for any and no apparent reason. This type of woman is unsafe and unstable. I pray that if you see yourself in this chapter, that you would take actions to purge yourself of this undesirable personality trait. It can do you no good, and it will only cause you grief. It can cause you to lose your husband.

Proverbs 25:24

It is better to live in a corner of the housetop than in a house shared with a quarrelsome wife.

I want to shed light on these things because when we finally see how we as wives burnish in the light of truth, we can understand how awful we must look to our husbands. This understanding can bring about a change into our hearts, which will bring a wonderful transformation in our marriages. Think about how you would like your husband and children to behave when they face the world. What kind of energy do you want exuding from them? In a stable home, children have the opportunity to grow into stable and positive spouses themselves. In a home where the atmosphere is set on God, a husband wants to come home. He wants to be near his wife. He wants to hear her and communicate with her. She opens her mouth in wisdom, and the teachings of kindness is on her tongue (Proverbs 31:26). Sweet words will draw him in (Proverbs 15:1). A kind countenance will keep him there longer than fussing and complaining will.

I am not saying our job is to conform to our husbands and lose ourselves. No. We find ourselves in the beauty of submitting to Christ by loving, respecting, and submitting to our husbands. It's a win-win situation. It is our responsibility to create a sense of peace and stability within our homes, where our husbands and our children can enjoy being.

MANIPULATION

Are you trusting or manipulating? Manipulation may be something we are accustomed to hearing about when it comes to wanton-type women, or a jezebel. However, that isn't always so. Wives can be manipulative, indeed. As unethical as the women with whom you don't want your husband (or son) to come in contact. I am not trying to put anyone down, and I really feel confident that we are in a healing place; therefore, you can be honest with yourself. You know what you are capable of and what would take you to the point of manipulating your husband. Most women do not like to be told no, and will sometimes do what it takes to get what they want.

Manipulation in the spiritual is witchcraft. The dictionary says that witchcraft is an irresistible influence. If we influence our husbands to do something by becoming irresistible, causing him to make a decision against his better judgment, then we are treading on thin ice, and could very well be dealing in witchcraft. It's a dangerous seduction that is in league with Satan. Why? The Lord does not want us to use such manipulation tactics as a form of marital communication. It opens the door to a negative force that will continue growing between a husband and wife until destruction is nigh.

The reason I am focusing on this word, as it concerns our actions, is because manipulation is a means to control or play upon by artful, unfair, or insidious means, especially to one's own advantage. A wife should have her husband's best interest at heart. The Bible says she does him good, and not harm, all the days of her life (Proverbs

31:12). So essentially, he (the husband) should be able to trust her (the wife). Trust that her actions mean him no harm. Trust that what she says is what she means, and there is no hidden agenda just to get her way. As an example, Christ humbled Himself and died for us in hopes that we give our lives to Him in return. He did not force himself on us; the choice is always ours to make.

Now, if we truly love our husbands, we would not want to seduce him in order to trap him. And if a husband is easily seduced and trapped by his wife to make decisions he knows he should not be making, then...*Selah*. More prayer is needed in the area of his walk with Christ.

CRITICISM

Are you content or critical? Another branch of a quarrelsome wife includes the very common action of criticizing. Criticism is an expression of disapproval of someone or something based on perceived faults or mistakes. What man wants to live in a house where an expression of disapproval is constantly hovering in front of his face? I'll tell you now, none of whom I know, and I don't have to know every man. The Bible is clear on this.

Proverbs 21:19

It's better to live alone in the desert than with a quarrelsome, complaining wife.

Most men desire to be respected by their wives, not to feel like a lowly servant in his castle.

> *Quick Thought*
>
> *Create an atmosphere in your relationship where your husband is reluctant to leave you and very eager to return.*

Constant criticism tells your husband that you disapprove of his authority, his countenance, or even his very existence. His home becomes a place that brings him pain. Eventually, a husband will despise coming home, and this is often where Satan brings temptation and places it on the heart and mind of the individuals in the marriage. The man may be the one to seek refuge, but at this point, either one of you is prone to temptations.

He will stay out with friends, make excuses to stay at work late, or find himself enjoying the company of a woman who doesn't make him hate who he is. If you want your home free of this negative energy, but full of passionate respectability...it can be done! Sometimes all it takes is for you to be quiet. I know it may sound rude, but I have a SHHHH that I have to tell myself when I find myself being critical.

At first, women tell me that they don't realize they are being critical. I can relate to that, because I didn't recognize it in myself either until I made it a point to listen and pay attention to what I was saying. I began planning my words

31

carefully. When I found myself starting a sentence in a criticizing manner. I'd quickly shut up, and immediately rethink how I wanted to present whatever it was I had to say. Tone and timing made a huge difference in communicating with my husband. What is "tone and timing" you ask? Tone is the tone of voice I chose, and timing is the time in which I chose to communicate. Merely being mindful of my word choice and how I said it helped me not be critical of my husband. The time of day, or even the moment in time is also crucial. For example, I quickly realized that I right before work was an unfavorable time to bring up any unpleasant issues.

It may not come so easy for you at first. If not, write down the negative things you say, and do. Rewrite them to be positive. If you feel comfortable enough, employ your husband to tell you when you are criticizing him. Role-play if you have to so that you can understand what it sounds like to him. If you have a good friend who is willing to be truthful with you, ask them about your critical ways and critical words. Have an open ear, because after all, you want to change this unfavorable habit and you want to do so quickly!

Ask Yourself

1. Why do I quarrel with my husband the way that I do? Why do I respond in such a manner?

_____
_____
_____
_____

2. Has he done something to make me angry? If so, how can I be angry and not sin?

_____
_____
_____
_____

3. What is the best way to deal with this problem?

_____
_____
_____
_____

Lord,
Help me to recognize when there's a battle going on within me.
Keep me aware of negative emotions that may cause me to
become quarrelsome. Help me not to react inappropriately or
become withdrawn. Give me patience, sensitivity, and words
that are sweet like honey. I pray that You restore my soul to
peace. I want to hide myself in "the secret place of your
presence" (Psalm 31:20).

The Quarrelsome Wife

ADDITIONAL NOTES:

_____

_____

_____

_____

_____

_____

_____

_____

BECOMING A PROPHET to Her HUSBAND

A prophet speaks divinely inspired messages. Prophets are regarded as having a role that promotes change due to their messages and actions. Is this not a wife's role in her marriage? Wives have the role in their marriage that promotes change due to their messages and actions. Okay, not convinced that you are a prophet to your husband? Here is the Word to demonstrate it. *So shall my word be that goeth forth out of my mouth: it shall not return unto me void, but it shall accomplish that which I please, and it shall prosper in the thing whereto I sent it (Isaiah 55:11).* **In the words you speak that are from God**, is where **you**, a wife, **become a prophet** to your husband. Choose your words wisely. They are seeds. If you don't want weeds in your marriage, don't plant seeds of discord with your words. For when you speak, you prophesy and speak life into your husband, or you prophesy and speak death. It is one or the other. Life and death are in the power of your tongue (Proverbs 18:21). Chose this day what life words to say. Be purposeful in what you say to and about your husband.

Do your phrases to your husband begin like any of these? If so, this is an indication that you are being critical.

CRITICAL PHRASES

You never ...
I don't like it when you ...
You always ...
I can't stand when you ...
Do I have to ask you ...

{

Quick Thought

Change your words, change your marriage.

}

PHRASES AND WORDS THAT AFFIRM

I like it when you ...
You are so good at ...
It makes me feel loved when you ...
I appreciate you, thank you ...
I love you just the way you are.

Psalms 119:11

I have stored up your word in my heart, that I might not sin against you.

Words are important, so speak life not death.

One of the best times of day to express your gratitude toward your husband is first thing in the morning or the last thing at night. The way you greet him in the morning makes him confident in being your husband. Have you ever told your husband that you are grateful to be his wife, or that you are blessed that he chose you of all the women in the world? If you have not, try it and see what happens. Give him credit for making a great choice in the wife he chose. Count the ways you love him, and then tell him. Find ways to praise his efforts throughout the day and week. Again, if you find this difficult, then look at the section "Phrases and Words that Affirm" and start with those. Say thank you often. Praise him for his faithfulness, and praise God for helping him to remain true to his commitments. Plant seeds of encouragement. Root out all negative speaking toward your husband, and you may be amazed at what will grow!

Quick Thought

Where does your husband go for adoration, admiration, and appreciation?

A PROFIT to Her HUSBAND

If you want to change or enhance your marriage, store up God's Word in your heart that you might not sin

37

against your husband with your words. You should practice saying nice things to him often. If you have had a criticizing spirit in the past, it may not come easy at first. That's understandable. Old habits are bard to break, not impossible. Don't give up. Keep at it until it feels natural. If he doesn't respond positively at first, that's okay, too. You may have caught him off guard, and he may be a bit nervous because this is something new for him to hear. No matter what, keep at it. The Lord is happy when we speak kind words to one another (Ephesians 4:32).

We must look to the innate ability and capacity to love and serve. This ability has already been placed in us. The principles are in the Word, and it tells us how to be the best wives and the best helpmeets we can be for our husbands. Proverbs Chapter 31 is perfect in clarifying what a wife should be. The Proverbs 31 woman is very careful to show admiration toward her husband's esteem and affection. She makes it a point to know his mind, to try to understand him. He leaves her to manage things because he can trust her. She makes it her business to find ways to do him good. (After all, God did say when he [the husband] found her [the wife], he found a good thing and favor in Him [God]. She above all, fears the Lord.

We should strive for this. Not only will we learn how to respect our husbands by communicating in love, but we will also find that when our needs are met through Christ first, there is no need for criticism and manipulation. We will be content in who we are, and we will be content in who God has called our husbands to be.

One of the oldest tricks of the enemy is to make you believe that your husband is your enemy or vice-versa.

Your husband is NOT your enemy. Satan is! Remember he (Satan) is the one who hates your marriage, and seeks to kill, steal, and destroy it. When the enemy attacks ... and he will ... you may find yourself bickering and quarreling. Stop! Think on the Word of God. It will give you wisdom and power to overcome the attack. Pray for your husband. The more you pray, the more God will change your heart and deal with his.

Ultimately, our relationship with the Lord is revealed by the words of our mouth. Words come from our thoughts, and our thoughts come from our heart. Our heart—be it sick or healthy—is a direct reflection of our relationship with the Lord. As mentioned in "Mirror, Mirror," when we don't feel good about ourselves, we have a tendency to make those around us suffer. It is a cliché, but there is truth the old adage, "misery loves company." The same can be said for those who are happy; they want to see others as happy as they are.

A wife has the unique ability to make her husband feel like he can do anything. A husband can reach his fullest potential as the man God created him to be when his wife believes he can. When you believe in your husband, he becomes secure, and he feels safe that he can rise to the occasion, and he can bear the pressures of life. When you believe in him and encourage him, he becomes empowered to do great godly things. You are his wife in order for him to receive the help he needs to do God's will.

Dr. Melinda Harper

> Here's an old joke:
>
> One night president and his wife decided to do something out of the ordinary and go out for a casual dinner at a small, not so fancy restaurant. As the owner seated them, it was clear that the First Lady knew the owner. She had dated him in college. The old boyfriend stopped to talk to them and exchanged pleasantries. He thanked them for coming to his humble establishment, and offered them the best service he could. After he left, the president looked at his wife and said, "So, if you hadn't married me, you'd be the proud owner of this restaurant."
>
> The first lady said, "I don't think so. If I had married *him*, he'd be the president."
>
> -Author Unknown

As a joke, this is quite humorous. However, let's take a look at what this first lady actually meant. She essentially said that whomever she would have married would have been president! She recognized her power as a wife and a helpmeet! She knew what her encouraging words could do for the husband that was put in her life.

How can your actions and words profit your husband? What can your words do for the husband in your life? What are some areas in your husband's life that you could you speak life into, giving him the boost he needs to soar? Being his helpmeet, what can you do to help him be more successful?

Proverbs 31:11

Her husband can trust her, and she will greatly enrich his life

Ask Yourself

1. Do I speak life into my marriage? Into my husband?

   _____

   _____

   _____

   _____

2. How often do I give my husband positive words of encouragement. Daily? Weekly? Monthly?

   _____

   _____

   _____

   _____

3. Are my words prophet-able and profitable?

   _____

   _____

   _____

   _____

Lord,
Let the words of my mouth and the meditations of my heart be acceptable to You. Give me the words that create a loving atmosphere in my home. Let my words heal those around me and not cause hurt. Let my husband's heart be filled with the positive affirmations I give him. May I be a prophet to my husband, therefore being a profit to him? I will tell my husband every day how much I love and respect him. I will thank him for providing for me and our family. My words will lift him up. My words are sweet as honey to his ears and his heart. I bring healing to my husband's broken places. I always strive to do him good.

Prophet/Profit

ADDITIONAL NOTES:

_____
_____
_____
_____
_____
_____
_____
_____
_____
_____

Dr. Melinda Harper

<u>CHAPTER THREE</u>

Controlling Your Emotions

 any scientific journals talk about the harmful effects unforgiveness has on the body. However, for the most part, people take this knowledge and put it on the shelf. Maybe for later use? I don't know. Only thing is, the damage is continuing its assault on the body, on the mind, and on the relationship where one or both spouses think that his or her unforgiveness is hidden or under control. So let's not shelve information like this, let's learn from it and apply it. Pay attention to the wisdom surrounding this topic so that regret and unforgiveness doesn't have the chance to weigh you down later.

Unforgiveness is harmful to the body...it has been researched and documented that these emotions can change the chemical balance in a person's body. Harbored resentment, bitterness, and anger can cause stress on every part of the body, including the brain. If you're not aware of the cellular or molecular damage unforgivenness causes, then we urge you to research it for your health's sake. In short, unforgiveness can cause premature death not only physically, but also spiritually.

Jesus does not ignore the fact that sometimes people hurt us. What he wants us to do is to stop allowing hurt, pain, disappointment, and bitterness to dictate our behavior. He says, "Come to me, all who labor and are heavy laden,

45

and I will give you rest. Take my yoke upon you, and learn from me, for I am gentle and lowly in heart, and you will find rest for your souls. For my yoke is easy, and my burden is light" (Matthew 11:28-30). We are not to return hurt for hurt.

Unforgiveness is poison! When we don't want to let go...we are ingesting poison, which contaminates our minds, and starts rotting our insides away. These emotions cause us to think stinking thoughts and can lead us into depression. It's a vicious poisonous cycle. Christ wants us to let go and forgive so we can be healthy and enthusiastically serve His purpose for our lives. He knows the damage it will have on our physical bodies, and if we are sick in our mind and body, we cannot do what we are called to do in Him. Satan would love for us to remain in unforgiveness and ultimately, to put an end to the purpose in our lives because of sickness, or worse—death. This is not the Lord's desire. He offers the restorative powers of Love, which is why He is so adamant about us forgiving one another. Follow His principles and you succeed, overcome, and win.

The act of forgiving has powerful results. For if you forgive men when they sin against you, your heavenly Father will also forgive you. But if you do not forgive men their sins, your Father will not forgive your sins (Matthew 6:14-15). As wives, we know we must be ready to forgive over and over again. This is why I can appreciate what Rev. Martin Luther King, Jr. once said, "Forgiveness is not an occasional act; it is a permanent attitude." I choose to forgive. Get rid of all bitterness, rage and anger, brawling and slander, along with every form of malice. Be kind and compassionate to one another, forgiving each other, just as in Christ God forgave you (Ephesians 4:31-32). Controlling our emotions brings order into our lives, which also means we are bringing peace and discipline as well.

This brings me back to the enemy and his plan. He doesn't want our mind or journey in life to be stable. The more negative situations he can force us into creating in our lives, the better. Most of us are liable to be out of control when we respond to the negative people and situations in our lives, thus, wasting precious days, hours, and minutes of our existence. Time is precious in God...look at all He accomplished in one week. He knows that we are capable of being extremely productive, causing a wave of influence to encircle the globe for His glory. He made us in His image and His likeness. He made us capable to do insurmountable things. Regretfully, none of this is possible if we do not keep our emotions in check. Yes, the Lord said be angry, but do not sin (Ephesians 4:26). Every emotion has its place. To every *thing there is* a season, and a time to every purpose under the heaven (Ecclesiastes 3:1). It is our responsibility to make sure they don't allow our feelings and emotions to get out of control.

Having our emotions under control not only brings peace to our world, but also builds a trust within our husband's hearts that is unparalleled. And this is what we want: for our husbands to be able to trust us, physically (by loving ourselves), mentally (by controlling our emotions), and spiritually (by being a virtuous woman).

I know that many, many women will take one look at their past and feel they are entitled to be unsettled, but this is no more true than the sun being entitled to burn up everything in its path just because God made it capable to do so. The Bible states that God has given us power, love, and a sound mind (2 Timothy 1:7). A sound mind is translated into self-discipline. With that gift waiting for us at no charge, it is ours to have forever–if we choose.

Bringing Up the Past

By bringing up the past, we take the scab off a wound that is trying to heal, and we pick at it. The scab is ours; it doesn't belong to the person who inflicted the harm. By continually picking at it, it might even seem like we don't want the wound to heal. It may seem as if we want to keep bleeding, thinking our pain will affect the other person. Well, it doesn't work like that.

For I consider that the sufferings of this present time are not worth comparing with the glory that is to be revealed to us (Romans 8:18). The Lord wants us to see what is before us. He has plans that are good for our lives. We have to stay focused on what is to come and not what has been. Like many of you, I too have been hurt in my marriage. In an argument, I was guilty of bringing up the past, thinking that if I said it over and over, maybe he'd hurt as much as I did. Sometimes I just wanted him to remember how it hurt me so maybe he could share the hurt. Repeating the hurt only kept it alive. I had to ask myself, how long was I willing to keep breathing life into this painful situation that happened? How long was I going to resuscitate the thing that almost killed me–that almost killed our marriage? What purpose was it serving to rehash all the details? The only thing it did was to revive the hurt and remind us both of the dark place our marriage was in. After reliving it, we almost always felt like we were at square one again. This was exactly what the enemy wanted. He wanted us to feel that we'd never heal; we'd never get past the hurt. He wanted us to become hopeless and sick. Hope deferred, makes the heart sick (Proverbs 13:12). Hopelessness can be one of the most destructive and painful feelings in the human experience. So, Satan tried to make restoration and reconciliation look so far off that hopefully we'd give up.

We could not go by what we saw in those moments. We could not trust our emotions. We had to keep looking forward and keep our emotions in control. With our emotions in control, we started speaking those things that were not as if they were. Confession brings possession. We confessed to having a healed, nothing lacking, nothing missing, nothing broken marriage. Today we possess a healed, nothing lacking, nothing missing, nothing broken marriage. Hebrews 11:1 states, "Now faith is the assurance of things hoped for, the conviction of things not seen." We (wives) have to keep hope alive and well.

Quick Thought

The wisdom in the Bible is useless to a person who refuses to let go of past hurts and pains.

Father God has plans for your marriage. Big plans. Satan comes to distract us with holding grudges, keeping a weary eye on our enemies, and putting up walls to shut others out. This causes us to be too preoccupied with protecting ourselves to even THINK about anything the Lord might need us to do. We become bogged down by sizzling anger, pent up hostility, and pressing health problems. At this point, we are in danger of not caring what our true purpose is in this life. Even if we care, we are too tired and too weary to do anything about it. Satan wants us to forget our roles as helpers and wives. He wants us to feel like victims and cry, "Woe is me, I've been hurt." Well, let the hurt go! Quit holding on to it. Stop replaying the hurt over and over. Change the channel. Choose to be the victor and keep your emotions in control. Above all, keep your mind guarded! Renew each thought, each day. Let the Spirit RENEW your thoughts and attitudes. Put on your new nature, created to be like God–truly righteous and holy (Ephesians 4:23-24).

When you change your mind, you change your life. I have heard it said, "You are today, the total sum of your thoughts." So what have you been thinking?

Romans 12:2

Be not conformed to this world; but be transformed by the renewing of your mind.

When God gets ready to change and transform someone, how does He do it? He does it by changing how they think. God changes the thought process. Be careful what you allow to occupy your mind. Take note of your thoughts. Your thoughts regulate your emotions. See, if you think on something long enough, you actually start to feel it. Once you feel it, you react on it—given the chance. Even if you don't have the opportunity to act on it, your body does react to it.

Let's test this theory. Just for the sake of humoring me, close your eyes for about two minutes and think about a pleasant time. Think about the first time your husband said he loved you or your child's first steps, the day you gave birth and saw your baby for the first time, a vacation trip, something you find to be joyful...

Did that memory make you smile? I bet it did. What was the pleasant memory? (Write it down so that you can always go back to it.)

_____

_____

_____

_____

You smiled, felt comfortable, felt loved in a sense. Your *thoughts* regulated your *emotions*. When you smile and feel the way you just did, something happens in your brain. Your brain throws a happy party and sends feel good messages to the rest of your body. Just the opposite happens when we meditate on negative situations and occurrences. Unpleasant memories rob us of having positive emotions. There is no benefit in negative emotions, yet we tend to dwell there far too often and far too long. We do not have to do that. We can think on those things that are good, and just, and peaceful. In essence, I am saying we are in control of how we feel in any moment. We are in control of our emotions; at least we should be because God has given us that power.

If and when you have trouble controlling your emotions, take a few minutes to do the exercise we just finished doing. Don't stop until you are smiling. Immediately erase any negative thought that comes to reside in your mind. Whatever is true, whatever is noble, whatever is right, whatever is pure, whatever is lovely, whatever is admirable—if anything is excellent or praiseworthy—think about such things (Philippians 4:8).

Ask Yourself

1. Do I become angry and irrational when I don't get my way?

   _____

   _____

   _____

   _____

2. Do I truly understand how damaging unforgiveness can be for my relationship and my *health*?

   _____

   _____

   _____

   _____

3. What is the best way to deal with this problem?

   _____

   _____

   _____

   _____

Dr. Melinda Harper

> Lord,
> I know you made me with emotions. Sometimes those emotions get out of control. Help me to control my emotions. Lord, I turn to You instead of giving life to upsetting, negative, or disturbing thoughts. Help me be more optimistic and see the beauty in everything You have made. I will not allow the enemy to take up residence in my mind. My mind is a sanctuary, and I will protect it by renewing it daily with Your Word
> (Romans 12:2).

ADDITIONAL NOTES:

_____
_____
_____
_____
_____
_____
_____
_____

CHAPTER FOUR

The Truth About Sex

ex was God's idea! Might I add it was a very good idea, too? Thank You, God. Regardless to what society says, God created sex for marriage, and to be enjoyed between a man and a woman. He knew what He was doing when He designed the body parts of a man to fit perfectly with that of the woman. God's intention for sex is for the husband and wife to be joined together and become one. It's not just a feel good thing. It is meant to build a strong bond between them. Sex is a private and sacred gift that God gave to married couples. Oh! Don't underestimate the power of sex within marriage. There are physical *and* emotional benefits.

Sex is worship! We glorify God by loving our spouse sexually. Sounds strange, huh? In the Song of Solomon, God eagerly encouraged the newlyweds to enjoy the gift of sexual intimacy. In sex, a husband and wife enact their vows, renew their vows, and in a sense improve their vows as they express and share themselves with one another and declare their love before the Lord.

Song of Solomon 5:1

I have entered my garden, my treasure, my bride! I gather myrrh with my spices and eat honeycomb with my honey. I drink wine with my milk. Oh, lover and beloved, eat and drink! Yes, drink deeply of your love!

Song of Solomon 2:3-6

Like an apple tree among the trees of the forest is my beloved among the young men. I delight to sit in his shade, and his fruit is sweet to my taste. Let him lead me to the banquet hall, and let his banner over me be love. Strengthen me with raisins, refresh me with apples, for I am faint with love. His left arm is under my head, and his right arm embraces me.

Like anything that is good, Satan comes to distort it and make it bad. Sexual intimacy is a wonderful gift; however, it becomes dangerous and polluted when positioned in the wrong hands. It is not uncommon for couples to have issues with sex. In fact, sex has been noted as a major factor in the decision of many divorces, so we see how important it is.

The world we live in is sexually saturated. As early as childhood, we are slowly being molded by the images and words that are constantly bombarding us in the media. Most times we don't realize the effects it has on the psyche until we mature. Yet, when we become adults, we have become a collective, walking expression of all those images, ideas, and words we were exposed to, whether they be positive or negative.

The world will tell you, "You don't need a covenant, you only need a condom. Use a condom for protection." From my experiences, a condom has never protected someone from being used or abused. A condom has never protected anyone from having his or her heart broken. The true covenant of marriage and having sex *only* within marriage is the way God ordained marriage to be. Sex within marriage is meant to protect you from all these. Yet, somehow, instead of listening to God as it concerns sex and marriage, we listen to everyone else.

Why would you take your Mercedes Benz to a personal fitness instructor for repair? Crazy, right? I have nothing against fitness instructors. They are great. They do wonders in keeping the body in shape. Are they necessarily trained to work on your vehicles? I don't think most of them are. They are trained to know specifics about how to get and keep the human body in shape. A Mercedes Benz body would need to go to a Mercedes Benz dealer, or someone who is certified to work on such a uniquely designed vehicle. With this in mind, why would you listen to what the world says about marriage? We too have been uniquely designed. If we want to have work done on our body, mind, and spirit, we should take it to the Creator. We should use the same protection with our marriage. We should take our issues, concerns, or problems to the creator of marriage—God. Believe it or not, God cares about your sex life. He urges those outside of marriage not to indulge in it. So, that tells me it [sex] was purposed FOR marriage. That alone lets me know that when my husband and I have sex, we are making God happy. We are telling him, "Thank you for the gift You has given us."

Healing from Sexual Sin

Many of us entered into marriage with sexual sins already attached to us. If we indulged in premarital sex, we have not only brought a sexual sin with us, but we also brought "ghosts" to our marriage bed. What do I mean by ghosts? Ghosts in the marriage bed are those thoughts, memories, and feelings that come up in the middle of sex that are not related to your spouse. Because we may have previously developed a preference, tolerance, and/or appetite for the kind of sex that we enjoy or dislike, we act and react depending on those very things. Even before entering the marriage bed, certain expectations are present. What happens is, if those expectations are not met, we tend to be disappointed or frustrated. As silly as it sounds, we are actually frustrated at the fact that we denied our spouse the privilege and right to figure out what we like as a couple, what feels good to us as a couple. Instead, we want our husband to make us feel good like "Joe" did during our sexual sin-capade, and that's not fair.

Some wives have told me that they would fantasize about that "one." Some husbands have done the same thing. It is not because you desire that "other" person. It is the appetite you've developed, and now you are married and still want that part of you to be fed. Well the chef who was cooking is no longer in the kitchen. Okay, keeping it plain, you are expecting your husband to perform like someone else, and that is unfair.

Here's an example of what happens. For a brief moment in preparation or even in the actual act, someone or some act from the past will invade your mind and remind you how you used to like it this way or that way. Sometimes, these feelings can be so strong that you visualize having sex with that other person while you are being intimate with your spouse. When you are one with your spouse, he can feel connected or disconnected. You are not fooling him no more than he can fool you. The disconnected feeling only happens because you and your husband **are** one!

When your mind is not in the act with him, you are not operating as one. He may not know where it is coming from, but he will feel that something just doesn't feel right. Men are less likely to act on feeling the ghost than we are. Because we, as women, are feeling creatures, we are much more in tuned to it. This intuitiveness is what kicks into high gear when there is a cheating spouse. Some women have reported to have seen, smelled, or felt the presence of someone between them, only to find out that what they felt was real. It was the evidence of a cheating spouse manifesting its presence.

Get rid of any outside interferences that can hinder your oneness. Pray the Soul Tie prayer in Chapter 5 in order to free yourself from any past sexual sins. You owe it to yourself, to your spouse and to God. If you suspect that your husband is cheating, pray the hedge of protection prayer over him. Seek God, and tell Him that you want your husband to be faithful like the Word says he should. Also, know that your marriage does not have to end because of an affair. There are things you and your husband can do to overcome an affair. There are thriving, healthy marriages that have had to endure and overcome this ugly act. Speaking to some of them about it, they say that they are much better after the affair than before. They are better because in getting help to deal with it, they learned more about what to do to safe guard against it ever happening again. The tragedy of the affair taught them some things about themselves, their upbringing, their expectations and ultimately their relationship with the Lord. If infidelity has not hit your marriage, good! These things still apply. Remain faithful. Surrender your marriage to God and allow him to fix it (whatever *it* is). He is the one who created marriage, and He created your husband. So, He knows what to do.

Sexual problems within a marriage are only a sign of deeper marital problems. Painful pasts can still hurt today. A cheating husband who you decided to forgive, having been molested or rape, getting an early introduction to sex as a child … all of these can create havoc in sexual intimacy. Get help if your sex life is suffering. Start here. Today, if we allow God to heal us, He will. Decide to be healed; declare that you will not hurt over the past any more and believe it! Decide to be healed from **all** sexual sins, and you will be healed. We are completely dependent on Him for the knowledge, the wisdom, direction and power for our healing. We want to be healed from sexual hurts or sins because a healthy sex life is imperative for marriage to thrive. He created us, so he knows what parts are missing in us; He knows what has been damaged. He knows what has been broken and what we need in order to be made whole again. He loves us, and wants to heal us everywhere we hurt. We just need to ask Him to do it, and allow Him to work. Let the Potter put you back together again and again if needed.

James 5:16

Confess your faults one to another, and pray one for another, that ye may be healed.

Do not deprive one another, except perhaps by agreement for a limited time, that you may devote yourselves to prayer, but then come together again, so that Satan may not tempt you because of your lack of self-control (1 Corinthians 7:5) When you deny your husband sex, you are committing a great and grievous act against your husband. In the book of Ephesians, the Bible tells both the husband and the wife not to withhold sex from one another unless in agreement and for prayer. It is only for a short time, and the instructions are for the two to come together again.

Proverbs 3:27

Do not withhold good from those to whom it is due, when it is in your power to do it.

Inviting God into Your Bedroom

Invite the Lord into your every part of your life, especially your bedroom. What? Did she just say what I think she said? Yes. The one place we fall short in seeking God is in the bedroom. I believe the reason for this has a great deal to do with our own perceptions of sex. Premarital sex would be one reason we would not want to see God in the bedroom. Many of us inherently knew we were doing something iniquitous and sinful. I encourage you to let go of the past sins, and see what pure sexual intimacy really is. God is happy when you have sex within marriage. That is the biggest difference of then and now. So, how does inviting God into the bedroom look? Well, you need to know God is not shy or ashamed. He's seen plenty of naked bodies. He knows what people do in the bedroom. Lest we forget, He created the very essence of it. We don't normally think about sexual intimacy as part of worship, but it is. Think about it like this. Your bedroom is a holy temple. Your bed is an altar, and you and your husband are living sacrifices. When you make love to your husband at the altar, you are reflecting God's design of the perfect love, and He is pleased. God is happy when you are "one" with your husband.

Pray with your husband before intimacy. Ask God to come in and make it fulfilling, enjoyable, fun, and exciting. Ask Him to guide your husband to the very spots that make you feel good. Ask Him to show you what your husband likes. You may be surprised at the things the Master Creator comes up with. Be open to it. Explore each other and don't forget to thank God in the midst! This is a good time to be a prophet to your husband. Tell him how wonderful he is. Speak life into his creative parts. Thank him for his love. Now is especially a good time to call those things that be not as if they were (Mark 11:23). All things, whatsoever ye shall ask in prayer, believing, ye shall receive (Matthew 21:22). You are truly "one" in this moment. One mind, one body, one spirit. Take advantage of the open portal of your husband's heart and pour love into it. If you want to solidify the moment, start thanking God for your great sex life immediately after sex. Something like this: "Lord, I thank You for this pleasurable time I just had with my husband. God, this was SO good. I am excited about him pleasing me and me pleasing him. Continue to make our time together pleasurable and exciting! Thank You ..."

Be reminded that God intended for you and your spouse to spend a lifetime learning what makes you and him feel good. Sex should always be in a state of evolving and growing in a healthy sexual marriage, so basically a lifetime is needed to do all the things you could possibly think of doing.

Ask Yourself

1. Am I fulfilled in my sexual relationship with my husband? If not, why not?

   _____

   _____

   _____

   _____

2. What does the Word say about marriage and sex?

   _____

   _____

   _____

   _____

3. How can I spice up the intimacy in my marriage?

   _____

   _____

   _____

   _____

Lord,
Bless our sexual relationship. Teach me how to be
affectionate toward my husband. Show me how to please my
husband and receive pleasure in return. Make our sexual
relationship fulfilling, enjoyable, and refreshing. Let there be
no inhibitions between us. Rekindle the flame and keep it
burning! Revitalize our sexual intimacy and make it all that
You created and designed it to be within marriage.

The Truth about Sex

ADDITIONAL NOTES:

_____

_____

_____

_____

_____

_____

_____

_____

_____

_____

_____

Dr. Melinda Harper

<u>CHAPTER FIVE</u>

Soul Ties

N the previous chapter, I talked about sex. I discussed things that could hinder sex in a marriage, and having your soul tied or mingled with another person is one of those things. I thought it was so important that an entire chapter is set aside for discussing it. Some of the things that are causing repeat patterns in your marriage are because of what is entangled in your soul.

The world tells us that sex is a hook up with no strings attached, and it is recreational. However, there *is* a physical and mental transfer when engaging in sex. Premarital sex is an indisputable way to end up with ungodly soul ties that hinder your current martial and sexual relationship. There are many different kinds of soul ties. I am going to explore the ones I feel are most important in helping us to become a profit and prophet to our husbands. The three I will discuss are birth, emotional and sexual soul ties. The Bible does not use the term soul ties, but speaks of it in terms of souls being *knitted* together and *becoming one flesh.*

1 Samuel 18:1

As soon as he had finished speaking to Saul, the soul of Jonathan was knit to the soul of David, and Jonathan loved him as his own soul.

Ephesians 5:31

Therefore a man shall leave his father and mother and hold fast to his wife, and the two shall become one flesh.

In Genesis, Eve was made as one flesh when she was created from Adam's rib. She was, in essence, born tied to him and having been created for him, they were one. When we married, we became one with our husbands. Sometimes it may not feel that you are one, but this chapter can help you get your "oneness" back by breaking any ungodly soul ties you may have that could be hindering your marriage. First, let's explore some ways that soul ties are formed.

BIRTH – When you are born into a family, there is a common connection that is established. Familial soul ties. Studies of twins who were separate at birth have shown that the twins had amazing similarities and traits. The separated twins in their adult lives were recorded to have made similar life decisions in careers, liked and dislike some of the same exact things such as food, style of clothing, and even music, all as if they grew up together in the same home. In some cases, they married someone with the same name, and divorced and remarried someone with the same name again. Extraordinarily, they even named their dog the same name. Coincidence? I should say not. They undoubtedly had a soul tie at conception.

Soul ties can be created by normal, loving, close relationships like that in a family. A mother/father and their child should indeed develop and maintain healthy soul ties. Healthy soul ties are important. These relationships are a blessing. They are selfless, seeking the best for the other person, and not concerned with their own desires. The Lord is pleased with healthy, godly ties. It is when the ties become unhealthy He is not pleased.

Overbearing parents, demanding in-laws, adult children who still act like children are all examples of having ungodly familial soul ties. Something is out of line and needs to be realigned in order for the family tie to be healthy. It is difficult to break any soul tie, but to break an unhealthy family soul tie, sometimes can feel impossible. I am here to encourage you that it can be done. From my own personal experience, I have had to pray and release family members in order for my healing to happen. Any kind of unhealthy relationship is not of God. God's desire is for us to be prosperous in all that we do. He calls us to love our neighbors as we love ourselves. Now that we have learned in chapter one how to love thyself, it will be easier for us to love others the way God loves them.

EMOTIONAL – Best friends develop bonds between them. People connect for different reasons. At some point in a relationship, a soul tie is created and that tie is what brings them to the point of being best friends. Some people connect through having common interests while others connect through having common tragedies. Trauma, pain and even shame can draw individuals together. Whatever the reason, ties can be emotional.

There are relationships that start out harmless, but can take a turn for the worse if we are not careful. We discover someone that we can share our thoughts and feelings with, and we in turn, find that we want to be in their presence more and more because they seemingly *understand* us. They don't ridicule us. We tell ourselves that they are easy to talk to. We catch ourselves saying things like, "He understands me" or "She thinks the way I think." Soon, we find ourselves longing to be with that person more than we need to be. If we are not careful, especially with the opposite sex, we could end up in a place of adultery. We, married women, have to be careful in the relationships we build. The one we should be confiding in is the Lord first, and our husbands next.

I am not saying do not have a best friend or a close confidante. What I am suggesting is to keep a close watch on how the relationship is evolving and growing. If you are talking to them more than you talk to your husband, or if you are spending more time with them than your spouse, check the relationship. Keep all of your relationships in their proper places. Test this. If your husband complains that you never tell him anything, or share anything with him, then it may be an indication that you are sharing more with others than what is needed. Have a person with whom you can talk to, but make sure you are including your husband in all aspects of your life.

Emotional soul ties can be linked to what someone has said to you in the past. "I will never leave you. I will always love you. You and I will never grow apart." When that relationship ended, you may have found yourself still thinking and reminiscing about what they said. You may have gone back to read old texts or emails. You found yourself daydreaming about what used to be and it hurt to think about life without that person. Why? Because you had developed an emotional soul tie. While we need and desire people, nothing should take priority over God's presence.

> ### *Quick Thought*
>
> *Who is the FIRST person you share good news with? Is your husband always one of the first or last to know anything about you?*

SEXUAL – The godly soul tie that is intended for husbands and wives is often distorted by the ungodly soul ties that were formed *before* we got married. Many times, we enter into marriage with fragmented souls. What do I mean by that? Well, when we've had sexual relations with other men (or women), we formed bonds or ties with them physically and spiritually. Our mind, will and emotions were often still joined with those we had sexual encounters with in the past. Physically we may not be involved with that person anymore, but the soul is still connected. Every time a person has sex, they become married to that person. In biblical times, the act of sex, or becoming one flesh was the marriage. In sex, you have been exposed to all the souls your partner has been exposed to and vice versa.

A woman who has been molested or raped has had a soul tie forced upon her. Often the woman feels ashamed for something that was not her fault. This is possibly the shame and guilt that was transferred from the molester or rapist to the woman. This horrible sexual abuse has been known to greatly affect later relationships, having the greatest effect on the relationship with her husband and with God if a healing has not taken place. How do you heal from molestation or rape? Keep reading, because there is a healing in your words, and in God's word. We are going to speak your healing today.

Many times, women do not share their molestation or rape experience with their husband. In some cases, the wife has revealed what has happened to her, and it was difficult for the husband to digest. In any case, we believe it to be absolutely imperative that if any kind of sexual abuse has happened to you, then you should share it with your spouse and pray the prayer at the end of this chapter.

Although sexual abuse of the past can affect a marriage in its current state, premarital sex can affect a marriage, too. In fact, sex before marriage has actually killed many marriages. Sex has been noted to be a factor in over fifty percent of divorces. Researchers have identified the most common reasons for divorce through a national survey, and sex came up the most. The lack of sex, too much sex, or adultery and infidelity…either way, a common theme in divorce is sex! I believe that sex is a common factor in divorce because too many people have sex before marriage. As simple as that. Going into a marital relationship already having found your G-spot, or knowing how hot breath on the back of your neck excites you to the point of an orgasm, is a pleasure that is denied your spouse and vice versa. Your spouse was supposed to be that person who "took you there" sexually. So, instead of waiting and learning what makes us feel good, some of us went into marriage *telling* and *instructing* our husbands on what makes us feel good (in the past). Based on what? Or should we ask based on whom? Some other man made us feel good (before marriage), and unfairly we set that as the standard for our spouse and for what we want in bed with him! The dangerous part is how often those thoughts, feelings and desires linger well into the years after we said our "I do." Resentments start to rise when your spouse can't make you *feel* like _____ did. Divorcees, whose main reason for divorce was sex, say this is when they strayed. This is when they started trying to find that old time feeling outside of the marital bed. Instead of ridding themselves of all previous thoughts, feelings, desires, and memories of past sexual relationships, they moved on to try to reproduce those feelings with other people. Sadly, this brings turmoil to a marriage, and often, marriages end in divorce.

Not all, but more than enough.

Moving Forward

We shortchange ourselves and we deny our spouse certain pleasures that only the two should know together. Unwanted sexual acts can creep into a marriage by one person or both trying to duplicate what was done during premarital sex. One spouse may have enjoyed oral sex before getting married, and the other never indulged in it. This split of desires can cause conflict when oral sex is initiated. It is also unfair. If either you or your spouse has participated in premarital sex, ask God to remove the images, feelings, thoughts, and memories of the other person. This is the first step to breaking any sexual soul ties and strengthening the ties that bind you and your husband together. God can and will restore your soul. To restore means "to repair, renovate, or return to a former condition."

> ## *Quick Thought*
>
> *Sex was intended to be explored
> in a lifetime—of marriage.*

Five Steps to Breaking Soul Ties

1. **Repent:** Repent of any sin that involves that person. If you have fornicated, committed adultery, etc. ... it is important that you repent those sins prior to moving to step 2. Be specific as you can. Some things you may not remember, but try so that you can repent.

2. **Forgive:** Forgive anyone who has wronged you. You cannot have any unforgiveness in your heart against the person or persons. Bitterness defiles the heart and hinders our prayers.

3. **Renounce:** Renounce any covenants that were made with this person. You or your spouse may have spoken words such as, "We will always be together" or "I'll never be able to live without you"

or "I'll never love anyone the way I love you." Renounce these covenants previously made with, or to someone else especially if you or he has said wedding vows with another person. The tongue (creating words) is quite efficient in binding the soul and is a means to create soul ties.

4. **Remove:** Get rid of anything and everything that has to do with that other person or persons. Holding on to such things as cards, gifts, rings, ... is an indication that you are still tied. Destroy all symbolic representations (if you have children with the person of course this does not include the children. They are a gift).

5. **Break it!** Verbally renounce and break the tie. The Lord said that whatever we bind on earth shall be bound in heaven and whatever we loose on earth shall be loosed in heaven. Do this WITH your spouse. I cannot stress enough how important this part is. You cannot bind and loose this on your own. You are "one" with your husband, so it would not be wise for only half of the "one" to take part in this. If your husband is not willing to do this, then ask your prayer partner or someone who will stand in agreement with you for your deliverance and your soul to be made whole again.

The soul is the deepest part of us, our spirit and innermost being. Since God is the one who made us, only He can restore us because only He knows what we truly need for our individual souls to be restored. Only God's Word can do it.

After you follow the five steps, pray a prayer of thanksgiving for deliverance, and continue to speak God's Word over yourself and over your husband–and children if you have them. Remember what being a prophet is.

Speak life.

Ask Yourself

1. Do I have soul ties that have been keeping me from being the wife I was designed to be?

   _____

   _____

   _____

   _____

2. Am I willing break any ungodly soul ties in order for the Lord to heal and refresh my relationship with my husband?

   _____

   _____

   _____

   _____

3. What are the godly soul ties that I have and with whom? How will I cultivate those and keep them in their proper perspectives?

   _____

   _____

   _____

   _____

Lord,

Forgive me for any soul ties I have made unknowingly. Forgive me for the soul ties that I have made knowingly with _____. I now renounce any form of ungodly soul tie that was meant to kill, steal and destroy my marriage! Remove any thoughts or feelings that are keeping me emotionally bound to _____. Free me so that I am free to be the wife You called me to be. Free my husband so that he is free to be the husband You called him to be. Let our marital ties grow stronger. Bind our hearts, minds and souls together. We are one because You ordained us to be.

Soul Ties

ADDITIONAL NOTES:

_____
_____
_____
_____
_____
_____
_____
_____
_____
_____
_____

CHAPTER SIX

Follow the Leader

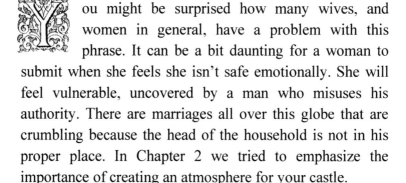ou might be surprised how many wives, and women in general, have a problem with this phrase. It can be a bit daunting for a woman to submit when she feels she isn't safe emotionally. She will feel vulnerable, uncovered by a man who misuses his authority. There are marriages all over this globe that are crumbling because the head of the household is not in his proper place. In Chapter 2 we tried to emphasize the importance of creating an atmosphere for your castle.

In the days of old, a king and queen mainly ruled castles. Thing is, these days, the queen is running the show, and the husband just wants peace. I understand how a household could evolve this way; however, it is still disheartening that wives are leaving their spots in attempting to fill the husband's role, and many husbands are submitting, or just graciously moving out the way and permissively allowing it.

In many cases, we don't know or have not accepted that we are helpmeets, a word we've been hearing almost our entire lives. But what does that really mean? Simply put, a wife is to help meet the needs of her husband. This is where most women fall short in thinking they want to be married. They never fathomed wanting to be a wife. When women express their desires to be married, we ask, "Are you ready to be a wife," and we get asked, "What's the difference?" In this chapter, the difference is finally, fully uncovered. Sadly, society has convinced women that we should be totally independent. There are independent women anthems, so to speak, that support this. These are songs written about being an independent woman, men not holding us down, doing life by ourselves, and being better off without a man. All foolishness. I wanted to share some of the irresponsible lyrics of some of these so-called anthems, but I do not desire to single out any artists. I am certain you can find them. You will see what I mean when you take time to dissect the lyrics and the meanings.

However, just to get my point across at how dangerous these songs and their lyrics are, I challenge you to stop reading and look up "Favorite Female Anthems" and see what songs and lyrics are revealed. Do these lyrics say what God says about your role as a wife? No. They don't. So it is dangerous to put the words of these types of songs on your lips, let alone on your heart. The messages these songs provide are not messages that promote marriage in the least. Allow me to say this, these anthems and messages are not for married women. These types of messages will ruin your marriage! God is not in it.

It's just a song, right? No, it's a declaration. It is a decree. If you go around singing these types of songs, you are declaring that you do not need your husband. Satan hears this, and you have opened the door for him to destroy your marriage. We must not give the enemy any place in our relationships. In a matter of words, you have given your covering [your husband] over to the enemy by declaring you do not need him. Be careful of the songs you sing, the movies you watch, the things you say, and also the things you think. Remember you are created to help your husband fulfill his purpose, and you cannot do that by being independent of him and declaring that you can do it all by yourself. So, independent, men bashing anthems are out the door.

When we buy into the untruth that we are our "own woman," we need to stop and look at how that is working in our marriage. If we are doing our own thing, and not including our husbands, we are setting our houses up for failure. Because many women, prior to marriage, have established bank accounts, homes, successful careers, and such, they feel that a man coming along is an added benefit to them. That is the reason so many successful women are still alone. They are not keeping things in perspective. Yes, as single women, we took care of ourselves because we had to. However, in order to stay married, we eventually had to make the transition into who we were designed to be. It can be very challenging, but it must be done in order to have a healthy marriage. It has taken me years of unnecessary struggle because I didn't seek God about it until it had gotten bad. It does not have to be the same way for you. This is another reason I felt this book would be helpful. We can save you years of heartache by sharing what we have learned. If your marriage is struggling because you are acting independently of your husband, then hopefully something here will help turn things around. Our marriage survived by the grace of God, but we know countless others whose marriages were not as fortunate as ours, and their marriages died a premature death.

Dr. Melinda Harper

As a Wife

Eve's sole existence was for Adam. Our sole existence is for our husbands! Before you call me crazy for even saying this, know that I too thought it was crazy when God spoke this to me. It did not make sense until I opened my heart and my mind and began to search the Word closer concerning it. The Bible is clear on why Eve (the wife) was created. She wasn't created to work; she wasn't created to have children. She was not created to be slave to her husband. God created Eve to **help** Adam. This is where her existence started.

I absolutely understand there is a sharp contrast between what society teaches and what the biblical scriptures teaches about the woman's role in marriage. The Bible exalts women. The world puts us down while pitting us against our men. The world did not create us, God did. So, what sense does it make to listen to the world?

Genesis 2:18

The Lord God said, "It is not good for the man to be alone. I will make a helper suitable for him."

With Eve's life being created with Adam in mind, think about how this relates to you and your husband. Declare right now.

"I was created with my husband in mind."

"I was created with my husband in mind."

"I was created with my husband in mind."

God has a plan for your husband. There is something that the Lord has placed in YOU and only you that will help him fulfill his purpose. Within the confines of your marriage, there are things that God is waiting to get from you.

Know that your marriage is not a mistake, no matter how you got together (unless you or he was already married when you met, which in that case, you need to be sure to read up on soul ties). In any case, moving into the thought of *I was created for my husband* is difficult for some to come to grips with; we know it will take some time and prayer. After coming into agreement with the Lord on why we are married, and to whom we are assigned to help, the work begins. We have to follow the leader. What does this look like? Does it give the man the right to treat his wife like a slave or a fetch dog? Absolutely not.

Let's look at the word HELP. In Hebrew the word help is *ezer,* meaning "aid." Aid means to care for, or to provide assistance, support or relief. The word MEET in Hebrew is *neged* meaning "counterpart or mate." The Biblical purpose is for the wife to assist her husband in life. A wife should do everything possible to assist, to help, and to push her husband closer to the Word of God. Remember you are designed to help him fulfill GOD's PURPOSE! You are doing this   for God.

Ladies, the assumption is if God expects us to be helpers, then the man must need help. If you are thinking, "My husband just doesn't get it right," guess who his helper is? If you are finding fault in your man, and he is not living up to your expectations, then help him. God said he needs your help. Our husbands need us to come alongside them, offer our wisdom, pray for them, and lift them up. WIFE … you are the ONE who was chosen to help mold and shape your husband into what God called him to be as a husband, a father, provider, and the priest of your home. Where he is lacking, find those things and infuse him with them. Look for ways to complete him. The Lord has entrusted this job to you. The wife.

1 Peter 3:1

Wives, in the same way submit yourselves to your own husbands so that, if any of them do not believe the word, they may be won over without words by the behavior of their wives.

Ask Yourself

1. Do I respect my husband as the head of the household? If not, why not?

   _____

   _____

   _____

   _____

2. How can I show more respect to my husband?

   _____

   _____

   _____

   _____

3. Would the Lord be pleased with me as a helper for His son (my husband)?

   _____

   _____

   _____

   _____

> *Lord,*
> *Give me the heart to obey Your word. Give me the wisdom*
> *to respect my husband. My husband may not do things the*
> *way I want him to, but let me remain patient. Lord, grow in*
> *my husband so that it will be easier for me to submit to the*
> *God in him. I want to submit myself to my husband like*
> *Your word instructs me to. I find it difficult sometimes*
> *because in my humanness, I see his faults and failures. Let*
> *me see him and love him like You do, so that submitting will*
> *be easy. Align our house with You being first and my*
> *husband being the head and the priest of our home. Show*
> *me where he needs my help.*
>
> *Follow the Leader*

Are you ready to be a wife? Now you are!

Forward March!!

ADDITIONAL NOTES:

_____

_____

_____

_____

_____

_____

_____

_____

_____

_____

_____

_____

_____

_____

_____

_____

_____

_____

_____

_____

_____

_____

_____

_____

_____

_____

_____

About the Author

My journey to becoming a wife was difficult to say the least. At the time of writing this book, I have been married for sixteen years. We have two beautiful children, two dogs, and great careers, and most people who see our marriage say that we make the perfect couple. Before I get into how much we were not the perfect couple, let me finish. Growing up, I always knew that one day I wanted to "be married." Although I had very few examples of wives in my life and those on television, all I knew was that one glorious day, I would have a husband. Like many, never did I consider what a wife was. I had no clue what wives really did, or what was required of them. I knew that wives had children and were responsible for them. I wanted children, too, but was I ready to be a mom? That's a different book.

I didn't know that being a wife was an assignment until eleven years into my marriage. Don't worry about doing the math, I'll tell you. Only within the last five years have I truly been a wife as a wife is meant to be. I'm still learning and growing, but I felt that this book could help so many married women become wives before it's too late.

No matter what stage you are in, in your marriage, you can become a wife.

First, I was blessed to learn that being a wife was an assignment. I had never known this before. I had never heard this, and after learning it, I didn't fully know if this was what I honestly wanted to do. This new knowledge that was before me opened my eyes to a huge, overwhelming and sometimes daunting task. I remember thinking, "If I had known all this prior to marriage, I don't know if I ever would have gotten married."

So, what happened the first ten years of marriage? At the time, we thought we were doing fine. We were an average couple. We loved one another the best way we knew how. People thought we were a great couple, and so did we. Looking back, we now realize that we struggled through it like most married, unknowing couples do. We were happy, then we were content, then we were fighting, then we were happy again. We went through cycles of love, contentment, toleration, friendship, and peace. Over and over, we'd do the same dance calling it happily married. I remember feeling there had to be more than this predictable rollercoaster. I asked my husband if he was happy in our marriage, and he gave me a resounding, "Yes!" This made me think maybe it was just my occasional down feelings. My husband once told me that all married couples did this. No marriage was perfect. I reluctantly started to believe it after talking to other married people who had no clue about marriage either. They meant well.

So, year after year we muddled through our marriage while everyone looked at us and openly exclaimed how we were "the perfect couple." We were FAR from being the perfect couple. Things had gotten so bad and out of control in our marriage that the thought of divorce found its way in and nearly killed our family—all while we were still doing our average married couple dance, and looking like the perfect couple.

I threatened to leave, while he threatened to stay. We were headed down that road. We were on our way to being a statistic of divorce. We were so close to it that I can still remember the feeling of failure I felt when contemplating where the kids would live during the school year. I also felt a sense of relief that now I would not have to do the tiresome "dance" anymore. I imagined I would be free. However, we did not divorce, even though we wanted to.

Meanwhile, our friends asked us to join a ministry called The School of Marriage Enhancement before we made any final decisions. I really didn't see how going to The School of Marriage would or could help us at this point. I was a stack of papers away from being free from this façade and farce of a marriage. I was tired, and he was unhappy even though he said he wasn't. In my opinion, it was time to let go. We both were very disrespectful to one another at this point, and our children were beginning to suffer the arguments and fights. We needed help quickly or else our family would undergo a great loss. Divorce is equivalent to death. Our future and our children's future were at stake.

The School of Marriage Enhancement

After the first session, we realized that we had so many misconceptions going into marriage, that we thought it impossible to repair what had been done. The first question we were asked was, "Do you want your marriage?" I waited to hear what my husband would say before I answered. After he quickly said yes, I followed. Symbolically, this was one of the first times he took the lead in our marriage. He didn't defer to me, he didn't look at me to see what I would say. He said yes without reservations. We both wanted to try to save what we had. It may sound crazy, but in the middle of our mess, this is when I fell in love with my husband for real.

The weeks, months, and years to follow were hard. I watched him work hard at making his wrongs right. He was committed to having a better marriage and so was I. We were becoming "one." We both had new revelation about what marriage was, what it meant to be a husband, and what it meant to be a wife. Because of what we learned, our marriage is better than it ever could have been. The things we learned in the S.O.M.E. classes are weaved throughout this book. I feel that my marriage was resurrected through these principles, and if my testimony helps you through your test, my test was not in vain.

The way the Lord has sculpted me throughout this journey, I cannot be undone. I say this because everything I tried to control or fix in my own way, never completely worked out. I refuse to go back to my way of doing things. I have learned to allow the Holy Spirit to rule over my mind and my marriage because He knows the formulas that make the chemistry of our matrimony work...in harmony. From the smallest suggestion, such as "tell your husband you're proud of him," to more serious ones like, "Pray for your husband in this season of temptation." He knows the how, when, where, why, and to what extent, and He needs a strong woman who can stand up when reality comes calling. I totally and completely trust the Lord with my relationship and with my husband because everything He taught me to do has strengthened, healed, blessed...and spiced up our relationship beyond what I thought was possible. Yes, we already know each other intimately; however, we no longer feel naked and ashamed in each other's sight.

Top Ten Things I learned from
The School of Marriage Enhancement

1. I learned that being a wife is an assignment.
2. I learned how to speak to my husband so that he hears me.
3. I learned how to love me.
4. I learned how to love my husband and children through their Love Languages.
5. I learned how to communicate in a more positive way.
6. I learned how to invite God into our bedroom.
7. I learned to appreciate the differences and accentuate the positives.
8. I learned that saying "always and never" is not productive in conversation.
9. I learned not to criticize.
10. I learned how to stay married and do it in a way that is pleasing to God.

Dr. Melinda Harper

LOOKING FOR MORE?

If you have comments, questions, or would like to invite me to speak or sign books at your event, feel free to visit me online, or contact me by email.

Website: www.drmelindaharper.com

Email: DrMelindaHarper@aol.com

HealYourMarriage@aol.com

Facebook: A Profit / Prophet to Her Husband

Twitter: ProfitHerHusbnd

SOON TO BE RELEASED

A Profit / Prophet to Her Husband
Companion Workbook

A Profit / Prophet to Her Husband
31 Days of Praying for Your Husband

A Profit / Prophet to Her Husband
Prayer Cards

Are You Ready to be a Wife? Before "I Do"

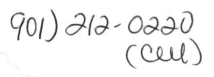

901) 212-0220
(cell)

CPSIA information can be obtained at www.ICGtesting.com
Printed in the USA
LVOW08s0615240415

435939LV00002B/2/P